To Rev. Thomas Saunders

compliments of

Bob Hallam

D1298556

THE SCARECROW SAID

Ordinary Seaman D/JX302754

ROBERT
KAY
HALLAM

THE
SCARECROW
SAID

and other poems

Stephen Hotel,
P.O. Box 571,
Whitehorse,
Yukon Territory,
Canada.

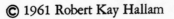
First printed in 1961 by the Press of Villiers Publications Ltd., Ingestre Road, London, N.W.5, Great Britain.

DEDICATED

to

My Father and Mother
> Who lighted a path for me to follow

to

The World Refugee Year
The Red Cross
> For their food parcels to prisoners of war
> and in tribute to the hands which blessed the cake
> that looked like a brick

to

The Rev. Dr. Stanley Russell, "Deer Park", Toronto, Canada.
Mr. Geoffrey Johnson,   Broadstone, England.
General Victor Odlum,   Vancouver, Canada.
> For their encouragement to the poet's pen

to

The Young Adult Fellowship of St. Andrew's —
> Wesley United Church, Vancouver.

> May the bloom of this fellowship remain fragrant in
> our hearts and in the hearts of those members who have
> gone to other parts of Canada, to New Zealand, Aus-
> tralia, Scotland, England, and Ireland. May our lives
> transcend in devotion to God and kindliness to every
> younger generation, that we may commit ourselves to
> God for the extension of his kingdom, the honour and
> upbuilding of the Church, and the glory of his holy
> name. Lord, you know the song of love and laughter
> in our hearts, help us to bring it to our lips and hands
> that all may hear and see, and know that we have been
> with you.

An Anthology of poems

Poems published in the following magazines

Australia — 21st Century

Belgium — The Seydell Quarterly

Canada — Canadiana, The Canadian Poetry Magazine,
The Dalhousie Review, the fiddlehead,
The Rovin' Pigeon, The Tower

Scotland — Allan Glen's School Magazine,
Kirkintilloch Herald, The Saltire Review

South Africa — Poetry and Prose

U.S.A. — The American Bard, The Avalon Anthology,
The Blue River Poetry Magazine and
Anthology, Chromatones, The Literary
Calendar, Midwest Chaparral, Scimitar
and Song, Starlanes.

I wish to thank the Editors of these magazines for their kind permission to reprint poems.
I also acknowledge my obligation to the following publishers:
Reprinted from THE PROPHET by Kahlil Gibran with permission of the publisher, Alfred A. Knopf, Inc. Copyright 1923 by Kahlil Gibran; renewal copyright 1951 by Administrators C.T.A. of Kahlil Gibran Estate, and Mary G. Gibran.
Reprinted from "Dunkirk" from COLLECTED POEMS by E. J. Pratt, by permission of the Macmillan Company of Canada Limited.
"Train Dogs" from FLINT AND FEATHER by E. Pauline Johnson published and copyrighted by The Musson Book Company Ltd., Toronto, Canada.
Reprinted from "The Prophet" by Alexander Pushkin from Avrahm Yarmolinsky: A TREASURY OF RUSSIAN VERSE, by permission of the Macmillan Company, New York, U.S.A.
I would like to thank the Director of Navy Accounts, also Bob who loaned me four of his photographs, Lily who found ten of my photographs, Ken for his proof-reading, all who helped me, and all who wished me good luck.

The Red Cross that reaches North, South, East, and West
    all over the world
       is fragrant like the dawn.
So it is with our religion.
It is either a small enclosure, or, it is a cross reaching
upwards, downwards, and sideways to the right and to the left.
Unless it is so we cannot talk of the brotherhood of man.

CONTENTS

PREFACE

I AM of Scottish descent. Though one of my New Zealand cousins claims our family is either descended from an Englishman captured by the Scots at the Battle of Bannockburn in the 14th Century, or, from a Dutch family who came to Scotland in the 16th Century, I have seldom thought further back than three generations and these generations are centered around Stirling and Falkirk. From Stirling came my father and from Falkirk came my mother. I was their fourth child having been preceded by a sister and two brothers who are now living in Glasgow, Guildford, and Baillieston, or, to be more exact, Stepps, Bellsfield, and Garrowhill.

I was born in Springburn, Glasgow, Scotland, August 11, 1921, and it was 1954 before I wrote my first poem in Goderich, Ontario, Canada. If the child is the symbol of the soul, and poetry is vision in the service of God, there was a fusion between my worldly life and my spiritual life at that time. I will try to unite both in this preface. I grew up in the simple little village of Stepps, five miles from Glasgow, where like the Spanish novelist, Palacio Valdés, in Spain, I enjoyed the beauty of the country as farmers still followed their horse-drawn ploughs and I delighted in the wonder of the cities, which throbbed and flowed between Glasgow, Edinburgh, and St. Andrew's with their immortal culture and heritage of the past. It was in Stepps that I sometimes jumped on the coal cart of the village coalman, who has prospered with the years, and whose brother-in-law, Willie Reid, won the Victoria Cross for gallantry. My "Three R's" commenced by my attending the village school where I was stirred by the stories of the early Scottish patriots, Sir William Wallace, the Black Douglas, and Robert the Bruce. From Stepps I gained a scholarship to "Allan Glen's", in Glasgow, a school founded by a carpenter. I later followed the honoured path of many physicists, chemists, engineers, teachers, and doctors, from that school to Glasgow

University where I graduated with an Honours Master of Arts Degree in Political Economy and Psychology. Among the older Allan Glen Alumni might be mentioned the names of Sir John Weir, Physician to the Queen, and Sir John McNeill, of John Brown and Company of Clydebank, builders of the great ocean liners — Queen Mary and Queen Elizabeth. Yet of them all, the carpenter, Allan Glen, who founded the school is the most revered in the hearts of all the boys who ever attended "Allan Glen's". My English and Language teachers influenced me to read the comedies and tragedies of Shakespeare, the poems of Milton, Lamartine, Musset, Lope de Vega, Pushkin, and of Robert Burns who wrote the vigour, radiance and humanity of life into his poems as colours from a rainbow. I read poetry for pleasure although the tone and rhythm of words and the harmony of co-ordination often eluded me. I was not aware that long ago Plato had claimed that poetry has no place in a reasoned society because it is not a reasoned pleasure. Poetry helps me to understand the people and the problems of today for it is a facet of history. It is imaginative, vigorous, penetrates everything, and is filled with the zest and delight of adventure.

Another University, much older than Glasgow's founded in 1452, of little beauty and without the music of the varied Scottish accents which I attended for three years was a number of prison camps as a Prisoner-of-war Guest of the German Government. After I left the hospital at Calais these camps included the Interrogation Camp — Dulag Nord, the Naval Camps — Marlag O, Marlag M, the Army Camp — Stalag 8B, the Air Force Camp — Stalag Luft 111, where I became an Orderly, the French Camp, Stalag 8C, the centre for coal-mining Arbeitskommando, work camp, at Kanau near Sagan, then back to Marlag und Milag Nord and the Merchant Navy Camp of Milag; to Marlag later came 400 civilians from Ilag Giromagny in the South of France.

This topsy-turvey upheaval came about during the 1939-45 War. One night I was a seaman in the Dover Gun-boat Flotilla of the Royal Navy, the next, only twenty-one miles from England, I was a prisoner-of-war in France. My Motor Gun-boat 328 was set on fire and sunk after an action against a German convoy. This naval night patrol of three Gun-boats

12

is one of the many engagements described in Peter Scott's book, *The Battle of the Narrow Seas*.

During these three years if the Red Cross Food Parcels stopped, life was more uneasy, and the diet was often reduced to sauerkraut and turnip soup. Friends were staunch and cheerful. Cigarettes and chocolate became a new currency for bread if retained during these lean periods. One lucky financier from the Channel Islands with a foresight of a millionaire traded cigarettes for chocolate and then accepted $20 or £5 cheques for a ¼-pound bar of chocolate. Security was unknown yet life for one aged twenty was an adventure, a struggle, and a challenge to be grasped with both hands. One of the preludes to poetry has been hymns, though not all of them are poems, yet one of the greatest to float as dreams across the water is the hymn of Henry Francis Lyte, "Abide With Me". These years might have been preparing me to learn in 1954 that, as today, the warmth of the past mingles into the present and that one is grateful for little things.

I remember Rabbi Goldenberg of Vancouver saying, "The interlinking of the part we play in helping the world to become a better world, through our decisions and our free will to make these decisions, is implicit and supplementary to the Book of Genesis, 'And God saw everything he had made and behold it was very good'. In the life which God meant us to live on the universe we either forward the process of fulfillment or we retard it". Set against the picture of war this is very true. By May, 1945, I had been a prisoner for almost three years and for the last month I had been foot loose in a camp near Bremen while as far as the Germans were concerned I was supposed to be on the march to Lubeck. The second and third years had been different from the first just as the first year had been different from the first month. Fresh and vivid impressions were felt less keenly due to assimilation, but a deeper asceticism and sensitivity had arisen.

Some months before May 8, 1945, when the war ended I began to see my first refugees, old men, women and children, all packed high on horse-drawn vehicles or on foot. They were Germans. Some of the 13½ million Germans who were to become refugees. In a very different

13

setting I had tossed bread into the compartment of frightened Jewish families going to their last camp at Auschwitz, a few of the six million Jews who were exterminated. A number so big it is beyond the reaches of the mind. I looked through my inner eye at these Germans and Jews, at the men on both sides who had fought at St. Valery, at Dunkirk, in Crete; the Polish girls who had taken messages through the sewers during the Warsaw Rising; the Russian prisoners of war walking on wooden shoes, or with nothing but cloth around their feet, always a thousand, a thousand times hungrier than I had ever been. Through them my mind's eye surveyed all of Europe and beyond. I saw houses ravaged by war — broken crockery on the floor with smashed drawers and torn curtains. I watched the housewife as she moved from room to room while more people came in to loot and rob. As I looked at her all that remained of war was pity. I went out of the house and looking at a little cluster of pansies I marvelled at the sunshine streaming upon them. On and on I went and then my eyes came back from a little German church in the hamlet of Westertimke, thirty kilometers N.E. of Bremen, near Tarmstedt, between the Weser and the Elbe, to the small Remembrance Park in my native village of Stepps where I used to stand as a child. So it was with all the people I passed on the way upon whom Christ looked with pity in his eyes as from their sufferings the Cross of Christ has more nails in it from the 20th Century than from Calvary. Nails which say, "Were you there when they crucified my Lord?"

God who knows even when a sparrow falls has heard the prayers of countless millions that generations might grow and know no war, that hunger and strife might be no more: the prayers of the early Christians for a world-wide Kingdom of righteousness and peace, the prayer before the Christian era of Pericles at Thermopylae, the prayer last century of Abraham Lincoln at Gettysburg, in that church of Westertimke I prayed my own small prayer on my first day of liberty. — May the world know the dynamic love of Christ. May peace, the secret name for Christ, become the heritage of the world for myself, and for my children's children. Though the future when "man abides in love" and "nation shall not rise up against nation"

14

may seem an idealistic mirage we have traveled far from 586 B.C., from the time of the fall of Jerusalem, when the Jews were carried away captives of Nebuchadnezzar, King of Babylon. They worshipped Yahweh as a tribal God of War, the Ark of the Covenant was carried before them as a Battle Standard. In time man may go ever farther in the search for truth. We glimpse the path of peace in remembrance, and then it is hidden from us till we catch the haunting notes of the Last Post and of Reveille, then we remember those who parted from us, and for us, in their glory, then we know that in the eyes of Jesus war meant a war against the Romans, an endless cycle of evil, and that we have the choice of either forwarding the process of fulfillment or of retarding it. In the words of the negro spiritual, "Deep river, my home is over Jordan".

In 1949 when I immigrated to Toronto, Canada, the war already seemed very far away for me as it did for two others from the village of Stepps. One, Jack Duncan, D.S.M., had been a prisoner of war in Italy, the other a civil internee of the Japanese. I became employed by the Ontario Department of Highways and came to know and love the cities, towns and villages of Ontario like those of my native Scotland. I can visualise the welcome in Goderich, Kirkland Lake, Niagara Falls, Orillia, Perth, and many other cities. I became a member of Deer Park United Church of Canada in Toronto in 1954, and a year later, a Canadian citizen. Yet having found the security of pleasant employment I am still glad that I abandoned it to return to the land of my birth because of my mother's illness. When I was a child my mother had instilled in me love and religion, she had influenced me by the pageant of the past, of Mary, Queen of Scots, of Kings and nobles, of freedom, friendship and romance. Above all she was very gentle and ever thoughtful. What it must have cost my parents in anxiety to have three sons at war — one a prisoner-of-war in Germany, another with the 14th Army in Burma and the other with the 8th Army in the Middle East, is hard for me to conceive. From my father I had learned of self-integrity, courage and industry. All his life he has been a skilled craftsman, and his main hod and hoe hobby is gardening. On the spiritual side I can remember the big Family Bible, the Sunday evenings when we

15

paused for a little while as children before going to bed. My mother was not a Margaret Ogilvy yet her spirit will be with me all my life.

After 15 months in Scotland I came back to Canada, this time to the West, to Vancouver, at the beginning of the 1957-58 Recession in the Canadian economy. By 1960, Greater, or Metropolitan, Vancouver had an estimated population of 770,000, in 1956, when it was 665,017, there had been 19,673 unemployed in Vancouver during December, in 1957 for the month of December there was 35,497, while in the neighbouring city of New Westminster the number of unemployed had risen from 5,525 to 9,205, according to the National Employment Service. I was one of the lucky ones to be employed, only to become unemployed in August, 1958, and again in August, 1960, for a little while. British Columbia was the hardest hit province in Canada in unemployment. At the same time it was one of the most beautiful, and the mildness of the winters attracted people from other provinces. Canadian unemployment mounted and by 1960, according to Hansard, the credit of the unemployment insurance fund had fallen from $852,729,261.78 in June 30, 1957 to $296,187,477.10 in June 30, 1960.

On leaving Britain I had hoped to sail on Mayflower II, to be one of the crew of 27 men, selected from 3,000 applicants, who wished to face the mysterious elements of wind and sea and the sense of a divine power, to watch the blue, red, orange and green sunrises, to go back over 300 years in time to sail on a beautiful blue sea with hundreds of feet of white canvas billowing overhead, or to stand breathless as the Mayflower bucked, rolled, lurched, pitched, and stumbled on a wasteland of water, then aloft like many a sailor who had sailed on the four-masted barques, Passat, Padua, of the great Finnish ship-owner, Gustav Ericson, I might truly sense the prayer of Sir Francis Drake, " . . . it is not the beginning but the continuing of the same unto the end, until it be thoroughly finished, which yieldeth the true Glory . . ." Yet like many other dreams and plans we hope for it was not to be and instead I sailed as a passenger on the "Laurentia."

In Toronto I had been a packer, a sanforising operator, and

for six years a Municipal Road Auditor, so, on my way through Toronto to Vancouver I called in at Parliament Buildings to see my "old boss," Howard Adamson. In Vancouver I was a book-keeper, I had a whirl with World Book Childcraft, I was a casual with the Unemployment Insurance Commission, and for a brief six months I was an accountant. From Vancouver I went to Whitehorse, in the Yukon. Time has gone by lightly, swiftly and gently. Yet the years from 1921, conceived in liberty, and dedicated, consecrated to the peace of the world through the League of Nations and the United Nations Organisation have not been light, or swift, or gentle for many. I recall walking over the hills of Norway with a boy who had been in Belsen. Later still I was to see former Hungarian refugees gaily dancing their national dances at the University of British Columbia in Canada. Canadians do work the world has need of. They have passports instead of ration cards and sympathise financially if they are able with the inspired incentive of Chris Chataway, the famous runner of the mile in four minutes, who with 3 other people wrote a letter of indignation that war refugee camps still exist 15 years after the war ended. Many have helped the refugees, people like Sue Ryder and Peter Casson, but this lay interest in the plight of refugees sparked public opinion and initiated the World Refugee Year. At present there are still about 30,000 war refugees in camps in Europe. People whose hope is that the broken fragments of their lives may be woven into a more abundant future. In this nuclear age poetry is still vision in the service of God. Yet vision is balanced by reason. Yet reason combines with resolution. Only by vision, reason and resolution can co-operation be balanced and it is for us in Canada to dedicate ourselves anew to peace, mercy, and justice as in the sands of yesterday it was the people of the past. In this rich, ever-developing land of Canada may youth glow forth with all its intellect, strength, and courage, so that with God's help, to-morrow, to-morrow, and to-morrow, co-operation may be achieved for Peace on Earth, Goodwill towards Men. May this little book, "The Scarecrow Said," remain a spiritual bridge between myself, the future and the reader. May the words unite with other words to conjure the hearts and minds of men for a renaissance of

17

poetry. "And God saw everything he had made and behold it was very good." What do the Communists feel about the universe and its exaltation and beauty? As the sun rises in Moscow or Peking they must feel the wonder of the Psalmist. When the Russians launch their space-ships they must feel as the Canadian poet, Magee, did in his poem, "High Flight." The dancers of the Georgian State Ballet may dream of a seraph giving a man a kinder tongue and a gentler heart as did Pushkin. When the dancers of the Peking Opera toss their red ribbons they may never feel the lack of liberty as did Lope de Vega. Who can tell? As the wild animals drink from the water holes in perfect peace so may the Communist and the Christian, the ordinary men and women of Europe, Africa, Asia, Australia and America, drink of the well of pity, the well that ennobles, so that wherever there is a call for help they may remember, "The world is my country."

FOREWORD

Yesterday is a part of for ever —
Bound up in a sheaf which God holds tight,
With glad days and sad days and bad days which never
Shall visit us more with their bloom and their blight,
Their fullness of sunshine or sorrowful night.

Susan Coolidge.

It is almost an intrusion to contemplate a "Foreword" to a book of poetry for, like a prayer, a poem is something of the spiritual rather than the material world.

Bob Hallam has been kind enough to paint the background of the thoughts reflected in each of his poems and, as the painter, he takes the reader on a tour of the gallery of his life. Each special moment of perception is framed in words — some reflective, some sublime and some sentimental.

In most of us our poetry is stillborn. We perceive and let the mystic moment pass into forgetfulness. Yet some are blessed with the patient spirit of the recorder and the thought is captured like a glass of pure water from the well of life. Those who take the time to stop and share the refreshing insight of these poems will not find it wasted.

All of the same clay, you may find in many a charm, a wish, or a sadness of your own.

Ken MacKenna.

THE SCARECROW SAID

The scarecrow said to one quite near despair,
"The time has come to wake from idle dreaming
  What is the use of tearing at your hair?
  A failure is a state of mind, but seeming
  Only a mood; rebuild and start by beaming.
  So take my suit to keep yourself in mirth;
  And soon, to-day will seem but shattered scheming
  The mist of memory in your rebirth."

The scarecrow said to one with little flair,
For meeting troubles, trivial or gleaming,
  "You should adopt an air, quite devil-may-care,
  Your brain will clear, ideas will come teeming,
  And you regain your proper self-esteeming,
  In thunderous tones that would awake the earth,
  And faith in resurrection roused from dreaming
  As memories fade out in your rebirth."

The time has come to wake from idle scheming
For all around the whirling planet's girth,
And soon, to-day will seem a shattered streaming
The mist of memory in your rebirth.

THE TREE TRUNK

Aft hae I rov'd by bonnie Doon,
        To see the rose and woodbine twine,
And ilka bird sang o' its luve,
        And fondly sae did I o' mine.

                              Robert Burns
            from — The Banks of Doon.

DRIVING A CAR IN THE LAST SNOWFALL

Through streets all white with falling snow
The corner is a snare,
The car moves crouching wheels to flow —
A prehistoric bear.
The windscreen wiper clears the glass.
The driver's face peers to and fro;
In wedge-like shape upon the mass;
The car spins round and fails to go
While children shout at it in laughter
The car is here for ever after.

THE VIKING'S DAUGHTER

Her eyes a sapphire sea:
Who dare their depths explore?
Impregnable the shore
To lovers, all but me.

We pledged felicity:
To love for evermore;
Her eyes a sapphire sea . . .
Who dare their depths explore?

The days dance by in glee
And beauty guards the door,
The soul and love are free;
Her eyes a sapphire sea.

FROM 7 TO 28

When I was seven my home around me lay
  Enchanted like a passing fairy spell,
To be enfolded by each new-born day
  The house was hidden in a little dell
    With scarlet roof bestowing joy to space
    To bring some laughter to the shining face.
      But I, at seven, in mirth did not suppose
      That life would have less beauty than a rose
        The years have turned some twenty-one since then;
      And mellow days are scattered to disclose
      That home remains a legacy to men.

At fourteen life was still all song and play;
  I climbed the village trees where many fell,
And from the highest bough I could survey
  The carving of my name on bark, to tell
    A later generation of the race
    Between myself and time, and just in case
      No riches came to me, that life bestows
      A royal epitaph as autumn strows
        The restless forest leaves throughout the glen,
      And fame is not the only thing which shows:
      "That home remains a legacy of men."

At twenty-one the fates took me away
  To war at sea and all was far from well.
The ship afire, the crew had to obey
  The order which to all was like a knell;
    "Abandon ship!" The firing ceased, by grace
    Some lived. But all would not return to base.
      While I could think of hours apart from those,
      For when in icy water no man trows
        That surly bonds of prison camps are when
      The lonely years are lessened as one knows:
      That home remains a legacy to men.

*The Growth of a Beard on the
Vik-Voss Road, Sogne Fjord,
Norway*

I

Cactii in my father's Greenhouse.

II

"Bemersyde", Stepps, Scotland, where my father and mother brought up their family.

III

Sandbostal, a camp near Marlag and Milag Nord.

IV

Four Boats of the Dover Gun-Boat Flotilla, M.G.B 328 being the near outside one

V

The cast of "Twinkle, Twinkle, Mr. Starr" with Talbot Rothwell (Writer-Producer) at Stalag Luft III

Malcolm Freegard, on the right, as Clemence Trust in "Twinkle, Twinkle, Mr. Starr" at Stalag Luft III.

VI

Malcolm Freegard as Aunt Abbie in "Arsenic and Old Lace" at Stalag Luft III.

"Tony Draws a Horse" Members of the cast of one of the "super" plays produced at Stalag Luft III.

VII

Master of Arts with Honours

VIII

Then peace arrived and lighted life to pay
  The living for the ones who fell by shell,
Or bomb, and now lay buried in the clay.
    While I, released to flee a prison cell,
      Returned to tread again a student's pace;
        And from my past embattled state could trace
          At twenty-eight another land which flows
          Unchained by man. With strength of youth I chose
            To live in Canada; and with my pen
          To testify amid the winter snows,
            That home remains a legacy to men.

ON MY 35 BIRTHDAY

At thirty-five I have a word to say:
  I came three thousand miles, as ties compel
That so I do, to see the church that may
  Be claimed by God for Saint Columba's bell;
      And there I learned that craftsmen often chase
        Their thoughts from wealth, to work as fine as lace
          In stone. The mind moves back. It glides and throws
          The memories of childhood which it blows
            As nerve cells tauten from the brain's quick den.
          My destined study for to-morrow goes:
            That home remains a legacy to men.

It seems the miracle of life now grows
High in the sunlit past, as childhood sows
  From parents, who may reach four score and ten;
The sanctity of friendly shelter owes
  Home its eternal legacy to men.

THE TREE TRUNK

One day I saw a tree upon the sand.
The sea had bleached it white and hard as stone,
I raised it up to stand again with pride
Stalwart, against the water's ebb and flow.
It stood a figurehead from out the past,
It could have thrilled a noble Viking ship
To sail the seas, but now it only stood,
Forlorn, with trace of what its strength had been.

THE SECOND SIGHT OF THE GAEL

"Good day! Good night!" breathed the briar rose
Opening her petals with a smile.
"Bon jour! Belle nuit!" trilled the French rose,
"Soon you will wear the latest style."
"Guten Morgen!" sang the German rose,
"We will waltz another mile!"
"Buenas noches! danced the Spanish rose,
Brightly coloured, free of guile.
"Youth! Youth! Youth!" said the Scottish rose,
"The bloom will only last awhile;
  So smile, and trill, and sing and dance,
  With every changing circumstance."

TO A FRIEND

I did not think when last I saw your strength and skill
Which gained for you the hard clay, sun-lit tennis fame;
In other sports of youth you challenged every thrill
With eager feet afire to speed the joyous game;

I did not think that you would ever lose the place
Acquired through many years that passed care-free,
And now, your mind contesting polio's swift pace,
You run an undimmed race for strength in mastery.

THE ELECTRIC CLOCK

The electric clock has no tick-tock.
The minutes hurry over
Irresistibly in the power of electricity,
As long as the current flows.
When it stops —
The old spring clock is wound and goes,
Tick-tock, Tick-tock, Tick-tock,
Clock and electricity are one
So heart and man unite together,
And the lost tick-tock cannot be redeemed
By the winding of an old spring clock;
Which goes — Tick-tock, Tick-tock, Tick-tock.

BALLAD OF SNOW AND MICE

The snow-plough clanks along the road,
A yellow frame is her spring mode,
Back and forth it rolls, and hews
With blade the ice-bound snow, then spews
It forth in broken chunks on fields,
Where snowy undulation yields
In ridge-like waves as trees await
Spring-time, gaunt in mystic fate.

The telephone poles now stand above
The stumps of trees and sapling love;
The trunks are motionless at rest
Amid the final snowy test.

The subtle mystery of change:
The orchard vines which now arrange
Their crouching arms as if in prayer
For rushing sap and fibrous hair . . .

Their arms outstretched in supplication,
While snow awaits the affirmation
From warmth of Spring to give them alms,
Till snow will melt around the palms,
And heat the rows of knotted frames
Around which children play their games,
To leave their footprints in the snow,
Or watch the stones as waters flow.

Now the dimensional depth appears
Around the tall and leafless trees,
Different in snow and leafy fringe
When branches furzed with buds will hinge,
Instead of shards of falling ice
Men hear the crackling sound of mice.

SMOKE COILS OUT

Smoke coils out in snow-capped error,
Black and white and fringed with fire,
Gushing to the sky in terror
From the village church and spire.

From the hydrant comes the water,
Through the bulging snake-like hose,
And the people stand and chatter
Round the fire and grow verbose.

Those who watch in cold are sadder,
Than the firemen in the hall;
Smoke conceals the aerial ladder
High above the burning wall.

From the roof where flame still lingers.
There the firemen start the search,
In the cold that chills the fingers
Round the mottled fiery church.

With the night of no returning
There has been a heavy loss,
And the people watch the burning
In the glow around the Cross.

THE EVOLUTION OF FLYING SAUCERS

The field of pumpkins sloped towards the road,
   Where now and then a Martian stopped to gaze
   At the red flashing splendour now ablaze
In spectral fire on every wagon load.
The autumn bringing frost had come to goad
   The mellow veins of leaves now in a maze —
   Once green, then red or pink or purple-haze,
That dyed the spectrum with a dark-blue woad.

The visitor from Mars had reached this place,
   A flying saucer was his spacious home
      For days, until the earth had filled the void,
This pioneer from cosmic, outer space
   Had stayed to watch the ways of man and roam
      On earth as if it were an asteroid.

THE CORONATION

I see the scarlet, blue and gold —
The pageantry from over-seas.
Combine the past! Unite the old,
And from all distant peripheries
To Princess Elizabeth fly
With prayerful homage on the breeze!
Beyond the sight of human eye,
Enthroned as Queen to pray and hear,
The souls beyond the upper sky,
A host which echoes in her ear,
"Good statesmanship has nought to fear!"

THE FLORAL YEAR

The snowdrop heralded
The January change in weather,
A cold white frosty month of bright clear hope.

The daffodil trilled
The boisterous March,
A yellow month of unrequited love.

The poppy flamed
The slumbering June
A crimson month of visioned consolation.

The saffron cheered
The September lure,
A golden month when the heat is past.

The mistletoe glowed
December is kind —
An olive month to challenge dissonance.

AFTER THE CORONATION

Elizabeth was crowned, and all that night
       The people danced on tireless eager feet,
       Contingents blazed in pyrotechnic light.
       The Cockney and the Ghurka in the heat,
       Both were in stature greater than the sun,
       They sang with beauties whom they chanced to meet;
       Indomitable London, bombs could not stun,
       Behind the kindly cliffs, an ancient host
       To Fiji Islanders who laugh and run,
       The white, the black, the brown, the humble ghost,
       Had come to honour One they loved the most.

TO LIVE LIKE THE PRIMEVAL MAN

The traffic lights below the hill turn green and red
And seem like dots to those who from the towns have fled;
The skiers live like the primeval man in joy
Of sight and stamina, the hope of girl and boy.
In cold that circulates the blood and makes them glad
Of wind-proof clothes, that insulates the body clad
For warmth, yet light like icicles that hang from trees.
The candlesticks of drifting snow that covers knees
Are contoured by the wind as sand by waves, in lines
That crunch when stepped upon as skiers pass the pines.
The skiers climb the hills like neanderthal man
Who realized that food was all he had to plan.

TO A BUTTERFLY

Dear butterfly
Drifting in flight,
Why did you have to die?
Red lapping wings flame bright!
Oh, could you not have swept them high
Over the speeding car, and up, and out of sight?

MEDITATIONS ON REMEMBRANCE DAY
AT NIAGARA FALLS

Millenniums it had taken to make their stock.
Piltdown hung on the frontals of their fathers.
They had lain as sacrifices
Upon the mortuary slabs of Stonehenge.
Their souls had come to birth out of their racial myths.
The sea was their school; the storm, their friend . . .

The Junior partner, Davie Scott,
Of MacTavish, MacEachern, MacGregor, and Scott,
Conspired with Murdoch, MacNutt and MacPhail
To go to Gravesend that evening and sail
For the Beach in Mr. MacTavish's yacht.

E. J. Pratt.

From — Dunkirk.

THE STRENGTH OF VLADIMIR

I laugh at night as wind blows north and south,
To bring the breath of God to the dark pit,
The prison camp; to say as He had taught,
Forgive! As I may be forgiven too!
My soul still free, the mind is marked with scars,
And joints now swell from lack of nourishment,
My voice is broken from long solitude
And in the evil weight that falls to shame
Through tears and wrath, my strength of will remains
As men, like beasts, get brands on arms or thighs.
The burning hate that stains their path as slaves,
With yoke and club to hedge their plodding way.
No matter what the future holds for me;
As people long for death I'm unafraid,
I know the nature of humanity
Through love of God: that life when lost is gained.

WOMAN IN BLACK

Woman in black, "God's will be done!"
Was what you said to soothe or stun
Your many friends who stood aghast,
That day the poignant news came fast,
That war had felled your only son.

Two years went by and there was one
With nerve cells taut, a foe to shun.
His ship was sunk, by bomb and blast,
Woman in black.

Once in the heat of noon-day sun
For him his strength had almost run,
And there you stood, still in the past,
And him you helped, as might a nun,
Woman in Black.

THE CREW OF H.M.M.G.B. 328

Casualties

HIGGINBOTTOM, Eric (D/JX345332). Missing presumed killed 21.7.42. Body recovered.

McNULTY, Andrew Doherty (D/JX284879). Missing presumed killed 21.7.42.

TOMKINS, Raymond Edward (C/MX67405). Missing presumed killed 21.7.42. Body recovered.

YATES, William Alfred (P/KX134142). Missing presumed killed 21.7.42..

COBB, H. P., D.S.C., Ty Lieutenant R.N.V.R. Missing presumed killed 21.7.42.

WALKER, R. L., Ty S/Lieutenant R.N.V.R. Missing presumed killed 21.7.42.

Ex Prisoners of War

BUTTLE, Alfred Leonard, D.S.M. (C/JX259253). Discharged 30.4.46. Home Address: 64 Mount Pleasant, Norwich, Norfolk.

CARRETT, Alfred Henry (C/JX258116). Discharged 25.12.45. Home Address: 289 Upper Grosvenor Road, Tunbridge Wells, Kent.

CHILDS, Walter Harvey (P/JX234138). Discharged 16.1.46. Home Address: 68 Darwin Street, London, S.E.17.

COLES, Leonard, D.S.M. (C/KX127567). Discharged 14.1.46. Home Address: 8 Normans Road, Sharnbrook, Beds.

HADDOCK, Reginald Robert (P/JX275271). Discharged 11.2.46. Home Address: 18 Stockwell Lane, Ayllihston, Lydney, Glos.

HALLAM, Robert Kay, M.A. (D/JX302754). Discharged 12.12.45. Home Address: Stephen Hotel, Box 571, Whitehorse, Yukon Territory, Canada.

HUTCHIN, Eric Charles (C/JX142128). Discharged 10.9.42. Home Address: 37 Weston Road, Huntsville, Sydney, N.S.W., Australia.

RAMM, Francis John (P/JX272799). Discharged 16.6.44. Home Address: 58 Dolphin Road, Redditch 1, Worcs.

RICHARDSON, Joseph Harold (P/JX313752). Discharged 8.4.46. Home Address: 66 St. George Street, Smethwick, Staffs.

JEFFERY, Arthur Charles Custance (C/SSX35125). Discharged 10.2.48. Home Address: 52 Bicester Road, Aylesbury, Bucks.

TUCKER, Walter William (D/JX232068). Discharged 9.1.46. Home Address: 10 Dalmery Close, Harrow Road, Wembley, Middx.

TAYLOR, H. R., Ty Lieutenant R.N.V.R. Died 11.6.54.

Let us remember those who drowned —
As coastal guns and star-shells frowned
The gun-boat spurted fire to knolls,
For the crew the year no longer rolls.
The savage, zipping tracers woven,
The green, the scarlet intercloven,
The shells crackled then burst astern
With flames exploding like a fern.

The piercing sparks no longer flew,
As she sank down without the crew,
For all had left the stricken boat
Save those who died but still could float.
And for the rest who reached the shore
The stars used all their sailor's lore;
Minutes of night passed by till day,
The dawn found life in them to stay.

The drowned remained in ocean land
To face the foe and hold his hand,
For birth and race are words of air
When death cuts down the young and fair.
And life glowed from the sparkling sun
Through depths of sea for them to run
To join the warmth, the light of heaven
In joy — a noble band of seven.

THE SANDS OF NORMANDY

White waves that fall in the rays of the sun
And children playing as they run
Bare-foot over glistening sand
Towards the concrete wonderland,
    Ivy-covered and mossy chained,
    As natural in time as peace regained.

They scramble over the single wall,
Play with their bouncing, crimson ball.
View acres of bricks and rubble,
Where men had hurried at the double
    To guns and planes that came demanding
    The bitter hours of the early landing.

The sun shines bright on children's pails
Reflecting the straining of white sails,
Ships, submarines, lumbering tanks
Gashing through wire on grisly banks:
    Crumbling churches and lashing seas,
    Red tongues of flames amid tangled trees.

They see no death in that quiet place,
There is no grief to mar a face,
They search for all the things that move:
And Christ once prayed in an olive grove —
    "The cup that was ahead . . ." The maimed and small,
    Recall the distant war for all.

LOOKING BACKWARD AND FORWARD
IN TIME OF WAR

The needle of the compass moves to star
The way to Sagan where the silence yields
To reverence the eighty who escaped
From waste of red brown, sandy prison-camp.
A wilderness of wire it seemed to them
With beams of light to aid the sentry's guns,
To tingle nerve and wrinkle trickling blood
Of men who crawled on hands and knees to reach
The shelter of the trees, to which was dug
A tunnel, all the winter and the spring
Through sand which crumbled down on men below.
Youth of twelve nations was there but to gaze
Across the wire as far as eye could strain,
And fifty sleep who gained their last release.
The sign darkened the camp when news was brought
That they were dead, were gone from earth to God,
And friends drew breath and thought of bombs on lands
Which would be built anew by those who lived,
As bugle notes went up and down and rose
To heaven and fell again to earth with peace,
A sound of hope that rolled across the square
Of silent men, in homage to the brave.
And now the compass stars the way to peace,
The peace that came to bomb-entangled lands
Where little children dance and sing again
And play in fields that once were prison camps.

The names of the prisoners who were shot after the Sagan Escape were pinned up on the North Compound notice board.

Flight Lieutenant H. Birkland, R.C.A.F.
    ,,   ,,   E. G. Brettell, D.F.C., R.A.F.
    ,,   ,,   L. C. Bull, D.F.C., R.A.F.
Squadron Leader R. J. Bushell, R.A.F.
Flight Lieutenant M. J. Casey, R.A.F.
Squadron Leader J. Catanach, D.F.C., R.A.A.F.
Flight Lieutenant A. G. Christiansen, R.N.Z.A.F.
    ,,   ,,   D. H. Cochran, R.A.F.
Squadron Leader I. K. P. Cross, D.F.C., R.A.F.
Sergeant   H. Espelid, R. Norwegian A.F.
Flight Lieutenant B. H. Evans, R.A.F.
2nd Lieutenant   N. Fuglesang, R. Norwegian A.F.
Lieutenant   J. S. Gouws, S.A.A.F.
Flight Lieutenant W. J. Grisman, R.A.F.
    ,,   ,,   A. D. M. Gunn, R.A.F.
Warrant Officer A. H. Hake, R.A.A.F.
Flight Lieutenant C. P. Hall, R.A.F.
    ,,   ,,   A. R. H. Hayter, R.A.F.
    ,,   ,,   A. S. Humphreys, R.A.F.
Flying Officer   G. A. Kidder, R.C.A.F.
Flight Lieutenant R. V. Kierath, R.A.A.F.
    ,,   ,,   A. Kiewnarski (Pole), R.A.F.
Squadron Leader T. G. Kirby-Green, R.A.F.
Flying Officer   W. Kolanowski (Pole), R.A.F.
Flight Lieutenant S. Z. Krol (Pole), R.A.F.
    ,,   ,,   P. W. Langford, R.C.A.F.
    ,,   ,,   T. B. Leigh, R.A.F.
    ,,   ,,   J. L. R. Long, R.A.F.
    ,,   ,,   R. Marcinkus (Lithuanian), R.A.F.
2nd Lieutenant   S. C. A. N. McGarr, S.A.A.F.
Flight Lieutenant G. E. McGill, R.C.A.F.
    ,,   ,,   H. J. Milford, R.A.F.
Flying Officer   J. P. Mondschein (Pole), R.A.F.
    ,,   ,,   K. Pawluk (Pole), R.A.F.
    ,,   ,,   H. A. Picard (Belgian), R.A.F.
    ,,   ,,   P. P. J. Pohe, R.N.Z.A.F.

Lieutenant   B. W. H. Scheidhauer, Free French A.F.
Warrant Officer   E. Scantziklas, R. Hellenic A.F.
Lieutenant   R. J. Stevens, S.A.A.F.
Flying Officer   R. C. Stewart, R.A.F.
Flight Lieutenant   J. G. Stower, R.A.F.
     ,,   ,,   D. O. Street, R.A.F.
     ,,   ,,   G. D. Swain, R.A.F.
     ,,   ,,   P. Tobolski (Pole), R.A.F.
     ,,   ,,   A. Valenta (Czech), R.A.F.
     ,,   ,,   G. W. Wahlenn, R.A.F.
     ,,   ,,   J. C. Wernham, R.C.A.F.
     ,,   ,,   G. W. Wiley, R.C.A.F.
Squadron Leader   J. E. A. Williams, D.F.C., R.A.F.
Flight Lieutenant   J. G. Williams, R.A.F.

In liberty is gold, treasure, peace and love.
                    from — Liberty — Lope de Vega.

Robert Lawrence (?), John Madge,
and Patrick Greenhous in "Arsenic and Old Lace"
at Stalag Luft III.

Summer time at Marlag M — Bob Hallam, fourth from
the left, back row, with Americans Otto Paulson, second
left, front row, Bob Thompson, third left, back row,
Ted Greer, third left, front row, and other American
prisoners of war on the left, from the ill-fated Mur-
mansk convoy, with Greek sailors on the right.

Winter time at Stalag Luft III. Bob Hallam and "Fish" Haddock on the right.

A snap of five British P.o.W's at Stalag Luft—l. to r. Lance Corporal Ted Tart, Able Seaman Bob Hallam—P.o.W. Marlag und Milag Nord No. 744, Private "Pop" Oliver, Able Seaman "Fish" Haddock— P.o.W. Marlag und Milag Nord No. 944, and Jack.

X

A group of six P.o.W's at Milag
Nord — l. to r. front row: Bob
Hallam (Scotland), Jack Dart (New
Zealand), "Fish" Haddock (England);
back row: Bert Elliot (England),
Marine Ernie Livick (England), Cor-
poral Fred Windass (England).
These pictures represent people cap-
tured in Norway, France, Germany,
Crete, Yugoslavia and the Atlantic.

A Sailor in the centre of six Soldiers at Stalag Luft III.

XI

*Scottish prisoners of war at Stalag Luft III. Bob Hallam
on the left in the front row with "Muckle Muir,"
Jock Orr on the right in the third row.*

*A Wing Commander, fifth from the right, and
"Other Ranks" at Stalag Luft III.*

XII

SAGAN

Sagan,
A small place to be remembered
Amid symbolic bombed cities
Of Warsaw,
Rotterdam
Of Belgrade
Coventry
Of Kharkov,
Stalingrad,
Of Chungking
Of London,
Air-raids in ratio as war blundered
On Hamburg,
And Berlin.

Fifty,
Small number to be remembered;
Twenty thousand died in cities,
Like Hamburg; in one hour perished
Hiroshima
Nagasaki
Sagan
A small place to be remembered.

"Sagan" tries to commemorate an event of the Second World War. Stalag Luft III, Upper Silesia, Poland; a prisoner of war camp from where eighty allied prisoners escaped in April, 1944. One got to Spain,
two reached Sweden and were flown home,
fifty —
including a number of Canadians —
were shot on recapture.

THE JUNGLE RAILWAY

The green periphery of trees
    Pinioned the prisoner on his bed.
        Gone was the peaceful span
Before decrees
    Of war brought to the watershed
        Reptiles and man

Lonely! No! In the part he played,
    On that railway in the defeat
        That shackled his stored strength,
Youth undismayed
    By tides of rain and weary heat,
        And rice in length.

In vassalage he built the rails,
    In a trauma from dawn to dusk —
        His fetters were now pontoons,
Time passed like snails
    On battlements of sodden husk
        During monsoons.

He knew humidity and ooze,
    He had forgotten norms but one —
        The cataclysmic fight —
What could war choose,
    Prestige, hunger, place in the sun?
        Peace dreamed at night.

Burma, Siam! Abyssmal rain!
    He worked outdoors in great distress,
        With guns burgeoned on tower;
Atoms campaign,
    And the railway ran in success,
        Alone to flower.

The dawn shines on the trees that come;
  Radioactive ruin that heaves
    The streets now torn and green;
Fire burns the home;
  Till at last among the leaves
    Peace flags are seen.

Glad was the lonely path he trod,
  That weaved his fears of death to quell
    The sacrament to be
To meet his God,
  And bid to life the last farewell
    Secure and free.

The jungle reclaimed to decay
  Folly meant to be eternal.
    The reverent cloistered ground
Cradled the bay,
  Where roses bloomed a wreath on all
    Who fell unfound . . .

THE CONQUERORS OF MARS

They walk the streets like amber ghosts
The boys from stellar wars,
Who dream of visionary hosts —
As conquerors of Mars.

For heaven is near and so is hell,
The graves are in between,
And when we hear the midnight bell
Their bivouacs are seen.

They writhe in dreams, they see the night.
They yearn for fevered birth,
They bring the key for peaceful light
To those who rhyme on earth.

The warrior boys are jocund ghosts
Beleaguered by new wars;
And some are poets who watch as hosts
For conquerors of Mars.

They recreate a world with words
Of freedom, work and rest,
And hurl aside the warring hordes
Of both the East and West.

They leave no bastions for the sight
Of nebulae to see;
But bards can hear through utter might —
The call to make men free.

They range among the baffled homes,
Invincible as stars :
Then crash the bells on belfry domes :
The conquerors of Mars.

DUTY TO COUNTRY
or, LET THE FIRES GO OUT

An army in trucks outside the city,
On which the snow rested in compassion,
As men watched the flames go out in pity.
Flakes flurried in the cold sun in sad fashion
Over stern fanatics, and laughing youth
Whose guns pointed upwards, sideways at the truth.

Pride wept openly, or stern and tense
At the endless columns of mud-splashed cars;
The city was condemned with no defence,
To accept the demand — let down the bars
Of fortifications — through other's fear
Of war or revolution, a price too dear.

THE ESCAPEES FROM THE PRISON-CAMP

White daisies lie in lonely hopelessness
On lifeless prisoners who sleep,
And know the flowers are kind to bless
The song and laughter they will ever keep.

Their slow death was not easy to endure;
To watch the once strong, sunburned bliss,
When idling death comes to mature
Their life, and lights the soul in the abyss.

Dark grey shadows have circled the cold brow,
Cheeks are sunken, and hands unbound,
Yet all their lips are soft as snow
In pure white dignity upon the ground,

And gentle trembling words are sketched in prayer;
Victor and vanquished walk the floor,
To reach beyond the depth, aware
That heaven is seen and lights a closing door.

MEDITATIONS ON REMEMBRANCE DAY
AT NIAGARA FALLS

Beyond a youth matured in tents of war
I wait for strength renewed to seek the past;
To wake again the bells; to reach a star
In constellations bright and vast.

The bells are peace, and three dimensional,
The past, to-day and time of unknown years,
The star is love, always ascensional,
Laura, to guide in clouded spheres.

The past reveals a love that dared confusion
Of violent war on sea and air and land,
And of the lovers and their sad delusion
That war could burn and leave no brand.

Both owned a loyalty one to the other
The love that came to each to light the soul :
But the war flamed, and then availed to smother
The love that peace could not cajole.

For those who part true love is unity.
A unity that neither faints nor tires
In separation, and a sanctuary
Of trust in God that love inspires.

    O death, is grief the victor of two camps?
    Or life for those who died that truth may live?
    Between two wars the bells draw near to lamps
    Of peace that gleam for man to strive!

The bells now cease under the linden tree,
Where thy name lives carved in my last farewell;
And all my youthful bliss is fused with thee,
It dies that love may trebly swell.

"Laura!" The name rings beauty on the air,
It brings to mind the dearest friend to me,
The spell fast woven in that soft brown hair;
But O the change in melody!

Ah blind desire to dwell consumed in dream!
The vital flame is past, yet stars still stand
Lighting the cherished name across the stream
Gold letters on a jewelled band.

Alpha and Omega have heard the note
Of fairy bells that dance with sunlit grace,
And the fresh springs of newborn peace devote
Their mighty powers to praise this place.

ELNORA AT 25

Love one another, but make not a bond of love:
Let it rather be a moving sea between the shores of your souls.

Kahlil Gibran.
from — The Prophet.

ELNORA AT 25

Elnora learned with warm nobility,
To be her tender self as mother and wife,
To billow joy in full facility
To charm her husband with her joy in life;
A dulcet mind, with grace to go before
Cyclic humanity, to know her share
Was to set free as through an opening door
Their tendrilled talent and their petalled prayer:
A minaret, to form the changing mind,
The wonder and the glory of this shore,
To bless with knowledge and with all things kind,
To garland precious love she gladly bore
A child, with dreams of chivalry and wings
To soar exalted while the cradle sings.

THE BIRTH OF SIGRID

Behold a mystery of charm and joy.
The mother's time has come; an empty womb
Now brings a melody that will employ
An hour that dawns with love to make a home.
The skilled doctor attends, gentle and mild,
Then prays with the parents, baby is born!
The bud that flowers to bloom the new-born child
A girl, noble, tender, life to adorn.
From springs of peace the white-petalled choir dreams
Rainbows, laughter, to tone a wider scope.
Thy name is Sigrid! and the eye that gleams,
The christening gift of all who come and hope
Her life will softly go, with God's care won,
Jehovah and Jesus, Father and Son.

TO ANN

When you were born with tiny tender toes,
Your smile was bright and eager from your birth,
And later on, when as a girl you chose
To comb your hair it tumbled down in mirth.

And you grew up to do a thousand things
Amid such homely laughter and applause,
Till suddenly your youth had flown on wings,
And people talked about, "The girl who was!"

A tumour on the brain! Was it a fact
That Samson's strength was bound within his hair?
Your photographs of bandaged head enact
Your strength was in your smile which stayed as fair,

The future years now quite unknown will close,
Yet all your friends will wish for you each day
(As when you were a child with tender toes)
For sacred gentleness to guide your way.

JEANETTE REMEMBERS

I wear a golden brooch, unique and real.
The heart of it records a withered leaf.
Once green when blown within the prison cell.
Its breath of subtle fragrance I could feel.

I had not thought the tomb of days was dead.
Yet all my senses quickened to its charm.
The eye was glad to note a lofty tree
Whose leaves were green in spring, in autumn red.

The hand was pleased to touch the strange dark line
Of veins formed by the One who made the stars;
The nose knew by the scent the wealth and price —
A Son upon the Cross. It was a sign.

And when the war had ceased, my husband bought
A gem to set the leaf, his love, and mine,
The suffering now past, though not effaced,
Our youth, the peaceful years for which we fought.

CASA LOMA

Out of the night and the north;
    Savage of breed and of bone,
Shaggy and swift comes the yelping band,
Freighters of fur from the voiceless land
    That sleeps in the Arctic zone.

               E. Pauline Johnson.
   from — The Train Dogs.

CHIEF OF THE FIVE NATIONS

Round Joseph Brant one snowy night,
The statue made of stone
That seemed to whisper with past might,
I walked an hour alone.

In eighteen twelve a Mohawk chief,
He fought with all his tribe;
And gained Ohsweken where in grief
He met with guile and jibe.

The tomahawk he kept in hand,
To guarantee, and seek
The peace desired by all his band,
Who waited strong — not weak.

I walked around and heard the sounds
Of songs, and then the roar
That seemed to say : "The meadow grounds
Have seen too much of gore."

Below this mass of honoured stone,
Two hundred years have fled.
Each passing year has cried, "Atone
For these, the Unknown Dead."

All men who live must learn alone,
That every country can atone
For heroes' names engraved in stone.

THE IMMIGRANT

He had left the frontier, and had reached his new home on
                                        that day
When the flowers of the Spring had prevailed as had this
                                        pioneer;
And though worn by fatigue, in his joy he then knew he
                                        would stay.
He had left the frontier.

There was peace in his heart, an ideal, hard work through
                                        that year,
And the hope to clear ground, for the farm to repay,
And, replete with harvests, delight both his eye and his ear.

As each things was improved the next generation would appear,
To rebuild, and to change, for expansion and power on the way;
For the lakes and the minerals, forests, and the new
                                      atmosphere . . .
He had left the frontier.

THE OLD ST. LAWRENCE MARKET IN TORONTO

The old St. Lawrence market-day
Was once the city's bright domain,
The centre of emblazoned play.

A thousand memories rise and stray
Beside the lake in sun and rain . . .
The old St. Lawrence market-day.

Toronto was beyond the bay
Where sailing boats and ferries reign,
The centre of emblazoned play.

Nostalgic planning haunts the way
Beyond the years that stir the brain:
The old St. Lawrence market-day

Where time is but a brooding spray
Upflung by space, a weaving chain,
The centre of emblazoned play.

Where shadows rise upon the clay,
And whirl before they flee away,
On old St. Lawrence market-day,
The centre of emblazoned play.

THE ISLANDS OF TORONTO

As men on islands of Toronto know
The yearnings of the needy for a beach,
A woodland park to watch the sunrise glow
On placid waters where the light-beams reach,
And when at dusk the crimson sun is low
The day moves on with tranquil, languid speech,
The people wend to houses in a row,
And time stands still for those who learn and teach,
So nature is a place where joy is hurled
Across the bay and there the city lies;
The happiness is seen for all the world
To grasp at night, as darkness pacifies
The poor who live in slums in the East end,
In every city where the stars ascend.

CASA LOMA

Casa-Loma —
A hill-top castle as rare
In Canada
As battlements grim and bare,
With high round towers;
A dream which made despair,
A millionaire's flair
For becoming poor;
A folly, erected with care,
Where hopes and plans
Crenelate like a stair;
A gigantic stake,
A fairy-tale and a dare —
A millionaire's flair.

CLEAR THE WAY

"Can you drive a little bolder?"
Said the large car to the small car,
"There's a lorry going sixty
  And it's growling down the hill!"
"What's the hurry?" asked the small one,
"You will reach your destination
  If you follow just behind it,
  Periscoping blind steep corners!"
Clear the way! The horns are screaming.
Crash! The cars are hurling down.

THE KIRKINTILLOCH AND THE OBERNKIRCHEN CHILDREN'S CHOIRS IN CANADA

I love to see the children's eyes.
    The choirs are singing merrily
They make me laugh if I am wise.
    The heavenly songs bring peace to me.

The choirs are singing merrily
    To dedicate the lonely heart.
Their heavenly songs bring peace to me
    In joy that never will depart.

To dedicate the lonely heart,
    In red and white and sporraned kilt,
In joy that never will depart,
    For they sing hymns of lyric lilt.

In red and white and sporraned kilt,
    They make me laugh if I am wise,
For they sing hymns of lyric lilt;
    I love to see the children's eyes.

THE CHILDREN AT MONT TREMBLANT

At Mont Tremblant the children learned to ski;
They climbed the hill to rise in ecstasy
In triumph over snow. They had not known
That speed of air and snow could deeply brown
Their skin, an atmosphere as bright as fate,
In snow which draped the trees to delineate
The ultra-violet light concealed in snow,
That shade on mystic hills in sunlight glow,
As, up and up, the slopes the chair lift flew,
And then the children skied downhill, and grew
Amid the atmosphere as bright as fate,
In snow which draped the trees to delineate
The ultra-violet light concealed in snow,
That shade on mystic hills in sunlight glow.

THE PIONEER'S FARM

"Arise, O Prophet, Look and ponder:
Arise, charged with my will and spurred,
The roadways and the seaways wander,
Kindling men's hearts with this my Word."
Alexander Pushkin.
from — The Prophet.

AN INTERPRETATION OF DESTINY

Clio, the Muse of History,
Mourns in the churchyard by the sea,
And from the cairns of Galilee,
A voice intones again the plea
That church bells ring in prayer to free
The minds of men of Calvary
That I may live with Christ in me.

YOUTH, TODAY AND YESTERDAY

O youth, you gleam for but a day
Of yesterdays, and reach the peak,
As a mountaineer climbs upwards
For many days, and then descends,
So youth is lost with downy beard,
The eyes of delicate snowflakes,
The radiant cheek, and lips that laugh
A little less each passing year.

THE HARBOUR

In ebb and flow the wife has known
That, come the spring, her man may drown,
Who hauls the lines of jib and block
On raft of logs from bay to dock.
She prays to heaven's mercy throne.

Her husband's faith joins with her own,
Between the cabin and that zone,
Anchor for both; a holding rock,
In ebb and flow.

The swell grows rough, a tree lies prone,
The Cape Horn gale all night has blown
Across the writhing ships that mock
As God then tacks for every shock;
She soothes her child, the anchor shown,
In ebb and flow.

THE BALANCE SHEET

In life there is a balance sheet
    The audit range requires transcendent tact,
The debits close, the credits meet
    With proteins, minerals, as iron fact,
For valiant men to fill the street
    With food and drink, before the fates transact
To buy with heart-ache, virile wheat
    Or charge integrity to counteract
The gap between, and help delete
    The serried need by some resurgent pact,
To reconcile, and to repeat
    The words of God — to hear, to see, and act.

THE PIONEER'S FARM

The Pioneer's farm at the clay bluff
Was carved by wind, and rain, and snow,
Maintained by horses strong enough
For two, but not for youth aglow,
To plough and sow.

Each path wandered in the sunlight
Past the covered bridge at the mill,
Where the robin, a tiny mite,
Swayed youth and flowering, flaxen hill
By the sweet rill.

Horses and cows were near the beach,
To rest in shade of the maple tree,
The chickens scratched the windfall peach,
And youth was awed by bird and bee,
On hill and lea.

And there youth learned the simple chore:
Kinship with God and the half-wild deer,
To walk along the stubble floor,
To spend one's self for other's cheer,
Throughout the year.

A POET'S DIRECTORY

The Allan Glen's School Magazine, Montrose St., Glasgow, Scotland.
> The Pioneer's Farm

The American Bard, Edythe H. Genee, 1154 N. Ogden Dr., Hollywood 46, Calif., U.S.A.
> The Second Sight of the Gael
> Jeanette Remembers
> Chief of the Five Nations
> The Old St. Lawrence Market in Toronto

The Avalon Anthology, Lilith Lorraine, Editor of Flame, Alpine, Texas, U.S.A.
> Smoke Coils Out

The Blue River Poetry Magazine, 104 W. Locust St., Shelbyville, Indiana, U.S.A.
> Ballad of Snow and Mice
> The Conquerors of Mars

Canadiana, Miss Hilda M. Ridley, Ontario, Canada. (address not known).
> To a Buttlerfly
> Elnora at 25
> The Birth of Sigrid
> Youth, To-day and Yesterday
> The Balance Sheet

The Canadian Poetry Magazine, Dr. V. B. Rhodenizer, Wolfville, Nova Scotia, Canada.
> Sagan

Chromatones, 1366 Dawson Ave., Long Beach 4, California, U.S.A.
> The Sinking of Gun-boat 328
> Casa Loma
> An Interpretation of Destiny

The Dalhousie Review, C. L. Bennet, Dalhousie University, Halifax, N.S., Canada.
> The Sands of Normandy

the fiddlehead, Dr. F. Cogswell, 495 Regent St., Fredericton, New Brunswick, Canada.
> To Ann

The Kirkintilloch Herald, Kirkintilloch, Dunbartonshire, Scotland.
> The Kirkintilloch and the Obernkirchen Children's Choirs in Canada

The Literary Calendar, Estelle Trust, 166 Albany Ave., Shreveport, La., U.S.A.
> The Immigrant

Midwest Chaparral, Mildred N. Dewey, 3302 E. Lee, Tuscon, Arizona, U.S.A.
> Clear the Way
> The Harbour

The Montana Poetry Magazine, Box 19, Seeley Lake, Montana, U.S.A.
The Electric Clock.
Pegasus, G.P.O. 1002, New York 1, New York, U.S.A. (magazine terminated).
The Tree Trunk
Phoenix, Ridgefield Park, New Jersey, U.S.A.
The Strength of Vladimir
Poetry and Prose, Durban, Natal, South Africa. (magazine terminated).
The Floral Year
The Coronation
The Rovin' Pigeon, Ontario, Canada. (address not known).
To a Friend
Saltire Review, 483 Lawnmarket, Edinburgh 1, Scotland.
The Scarecrow Said
Scimitar and Song, Lura T. McNair, Jonesboro Heights St., R7, Sanford, N.C., U.S.A.
The Islands of Toronto
The Seydell Quarterly, Brussells, Belgium. (address not known)
To Live like the Primeval Man
Starlanes, Orma McCormick, 1558 W. Hazelhurst St., Ferndale 20, Michigan, U.S.A.
The Evolution of Flying Saucers
The Tower, Miss Thomson, 880 Garth Street, Hamilton, Ontario, Canada.
Looking Backward and Forward in Time of War
Meditations on Remembrance Day at Niagara Falls
21st Century, Box 3015, G.P.O., Sydney, New South Wales, Australia.
The Escapees from the Prison Camp

POSTSCRIPT

What, Where, How, Why, When
for the
Person who seldom reads Poetry

1 — The Scarecrow Said
16 — Miscellaneous Poems
11 — War Poems
4 — Poems of People
8 — Poems of Canada
5 — Religious Poems
—
Total 45
—

NOTES

1. *The Scarecrow Said*

   This is the original idea though not one of my first poems and it was published in the very selective "Saltire Review," Scotland. It is a skit of three facets of the forces between the world, the individual, and the scarecrow, who like the one in "The Wizard of Oz," pokes fun at everyone even though he does not have a brain to know that the left hand side of the brain controls the right hand side of the body. There is something humorous to me about a scarecrow giving his suit to a person who has been overwhelmed with the pressures of life, who has practically abandoned hope and faith in the world. The first verse means that the memory of what has happened should not affect the present, or, endanger the future. The second verse is a more emphatic repetition, and the last verse implies that time will heal and cure even better than the Blarney Stone!

2. *Driving a Car in the Last Snow-Fall*

   From my window in Brantford, Ontario, I looked down on a cross-road one winter night and watched the cars stop, then struggle to turn the corner in snow over six inches deep. The drivers were less experienced in snow conditions than the ones in Sault Saint Marie. All of this was very amusing to a group of children who were watching from the sidewalk and who were supposed to be learning for their school lesson that baking-powder, aspirins and nylons are by-products of coal, or, to know the names of the five Jesuit priests who were massacred near Toronto in the 17th century by the Indians.

3. *The Viking's Daughter*

   Perhaps expresses the feeling, "Gentlemen Prefer Blonds." The word association interpretation might be that the two penny magazines, Rover, Adventure, Wizard which I sometimes read as a boy were often about Vikings discovering Greenland, the largest island in the world.

There is a story told that when a famous poet was asked the meaning of one of his poems, he replied, "That when it was written only two people knew, himself and God, now only God knew."

4. *From 7 to 28*
Is a biographical sketch based on the old belief that "7" and multiples of "7" are magical numbers in our lives. Again much of ourselves as adults is affected by our childhood in our parents' home. Childhood and early adolescence are depicted by verses one and two. In the village park in Stepps, in 1934, I carved my name on the top of four of the tallest and most difficult trees to climb. At adolescence nothing is impossible. Two years later I walked round the Island of Arran, 64 miles, in a day. Verse three describes the journey from the sheltered village life and home to war, verse four infers the return of peace, and the high hopes of those who came back with the desire to become civilians, to help the old and the young, the poor and the infirm, to find a cure for cancer, to reach the moon, to climb Mount Everest, or, just to lie on the green grass, watching children climbing trees like chimpanzees to swim, to ski, to love and be loved in a world at peace.

5. *On my 35 Birthday*
On my mother's illness I returned home to "Bemersyde," Stepps. I felt I could well afford from the viewpoint of time to spend some months of my life in visiting my parents. During that visit, unlike a previous one when I had spent two weeks in Paris, I spent two weeks in the Outer Hebrides and two weeks on the Isle of Iona where St. Columba had landed from Ireland in the 6th century, bringing with him the 39 books of the Old Testament and the 27 of the New Testament. This Benedictine monk built the monastery to which Dr. George Macleod took a group of unemployed for the rebuilding of the abbey during the 1930 Depression and so developed the Iona Community. All the Abbey lacks is "The Book of

Kells! While I was visiting my parents central heating was installed in their home. At "Bemersyde," I saw four TV programmes of "This is Your Life," presenting Sir John Barbirolli, Brian Hessian, Colin Hodgkinson, Sue Ryder. I would have liked to have seen a previous one about Anne Brusselmans M.B.E.

6. *The Tree Trunk*
This is one of my favourite poems. It was written on the sands of Cobourg, Ontario, one day after work, and was published in the United States magazine, Pegasus. The thought behind the poem is that some people develop their talents and attain their ideals, others less fortunate, dream only of what might have been, as futilely, as if they were wondering how much they would weigh on the sun where the sun's gravity is about 28 times the earth's if it was possible for them to stand there after travelling the 91,402,000 miles for 150 days at 25,000 miles per hour.

7. *The Second Sight of the Gael*
Languages have always enthralled me as a gateway through which I could pass to know and understand other nations. For that reason, from the 2,800, or so, languages, I have studied French, Spanish, and touched the fringe of German and Russian. Here I play with certain characteristics of people symbolised as roses. First the wild rose — beautiful on the country lanes, then the French rose of fashion, the German-Austrian rose of the waltz, and the Scottish rose of foresight, canniness and love of life, a rose long sheltered with apples and strawberries among the crags of Hadrian's Wall.

8. *To a Friend*
The lines of Shakespeare come to my mind:
I count myself in nothing else so happy
As in a soul remembering my good friends.
This poem was written for a great sportsman, stricken with polio, with whom I used to play tennis at Moore Park

Tennis Club, Toronto. When we were losing a set at doubles he would say, "Come on, we'll take this set." We did!

9. *Ballad of Snow and Mice*
This ballad is symbolic of the change from snow-covered fields to ones where the field mice run looking for straw to build their nests, and is set against the gigantic snow ploughs which heave and push and blow the snow from the highways like a pole vaulter jumping on the moon with its gravity $\frac{1}{6}$ of the earth's.

10. *Smoke Coils Out*
One day while I was working in Hamilton, Ontario, I saw a fire from the office window. Later, on that chilly winter's day, of Ontario's, I walked down the street, over the hoses strewn on the sidewalk and saw the devastation caused by the fire.
The same evening I chanced to read in the library about Sir Henry Morgan, the Welsh pirate of the 18th century, who had destroyed by fire one of the oldest churches in the Americas, a church at Panama built in the 16th century.

11. *The Electric Clock*
Compares the difference between the heart of man and the electric clock which goes on for ever as long as there is electricity.

12. *The Evolution of Flying Saucers*
A phantasy on Martians, pumpkins, autumn, and flying saucers on the theory that there is some plant life on Mars.

13. *The Floral Year*
Is to me a charming little poem relating flowers and their meanings to the months of the year. I wrote it lying on the grass while waiting in Toronto for the Centre Island Ferry.

14. *The Coronation*
    When I arrived in Brantford I did not expect to be reminded of Edinburgh, Scotland, but it was here that Alexander Graham Bell invented the telephone and I remembered his birthplace in Edinburgh. The "Y.M.C.A." had a television set and after I came out of the swimming pool I watched one of my first TV programmes — The Coronation. Princess Elizabeth seemed so very young for the responsibilities of a ruler. I later wrote the poem in Toronto.

15. *After the Coronation*
    Depicts my love of London, admiration for the Cockney, Fiji Islander and Ghurka.

16. *To Live Like the Primeval Man*
    Geologists say that the earth is 3 billion years old and that the earliest trace of man as found in Java and Peking is about 500,000 years old, that the earliest records of human history is about 3,000 years and that the earliest trace of primates is about 60,000,000 years. To-day Java is the most densely populated island in the world, and China has a surging population of over 650,000,000, and will reach 1 billion by 1980, the greatest group of organized society the world has ever known.
    Yet as I made my last ski-run down those exhilarating snow covered slopes I was merely a primeval man thinking of shelter, food and fire — a drink, a hot bath, a change of clothing, a T-bone steak, and the comfort of a fire.

17. *To a Butterfly*
    One day I drove down to Picton, Ontario, and on arrival there I found a little butterfly dead in the grille of my car. It seemed sadly beautiful as it lay motionless in the palm of my hand. I thought of Robert Burns inadvertently destroying the nest of a mouse with the blade of his plough and decided to build a little cairn in the form of a poem.

66

18. *The Strength of Vladimir*
This was one of my first poems experimenting with blank verse. I was influenced by Henley's poem, "Invictus." The first four lines develop the word "Forgive" from the Lord's Prayer.

"Get brands . . ." relates to the practice of tattooing prison numbers on the forearm or thigh of concentration camp prisoners.

The poem is based on my belief of the last line that there is a life after death just as surely as the moon circles the earth thirteen times a year and that the earth travels round the sun.

19. *Woman in Black*
Before I was taken a prisoner-of-war I received multiple gun-shot wounds in the knee, arm, shoulder and wrist. The day I left the hospital at Calais was my second day out of bed and I travelled 500 miles to Wilhelmshaven, mainly by train, a little by truck, and a little on foot, under guard, and at the end, I was just as exhausted as Mao Tse Tung must have been when he marched 6,000 miles from Southern China to Yenan. On the station at Wilhelmshaven I could not lift my leg to lie down on a bench and a woman dressed in black came forward and raised it for me. This kindness led to the writing of this poem as a tribute for the act of that unknown woman in black, who, if she had lived 20 centuries ago might have been Lydia, the first Christian believer in Europe, and said, "Grace be with you!" The reply would have been, "Peace be to your House!" With me too, were Stoker Len Coles, "Bunts" Carrett, and "Sparks" Tucker.

20. *The Sands of Normandy*
This poem was published in the Dalhousie Review. It is about an imaginary visit to the battlefields of Normandy by one who had taken part in the Normandy Landing. It contrasts the playing of children in the present with the landing of men, guns, and tanks. It compares their ordeal of fire with the ordeal of Christ who prayed that if it was

God's will, the cup that was ahead might be taken from Him.

21. *The Sinking of Gun-boat 328*

I did my naval training in Devon and Cornwall, Fort William in Scotland, then down to Ramsgate and Dover. On one of my last leaves I remember watching the pigeons as I walked past the statue of Horatio Nelson in Trafalgar Square, I strolled along the Thames and then the next evening I was on the sands of Dover. The sinking of Gun-boat 328 took place on the night of July 21, 1942. Of the crew of eighteen all were casualties — killed, wounded, or through exposure. As an Ordinary Seaman I was assisting on the starboard Lewis gun. It was probably the last to fire, which was very eerie in the still silence from our boat. During the action the German hot green tracer bullets had crossed the British hot red tracer bullets. The star shells overhead silhouetted the boat against the darkness of the night. At the beginning it seemed a strangely beautiful remote scene as were the blue, red and green sparkling flares which later I was to see dropped to pinpoint targets in Bremen, Kiel, and Cuxhaven for phosphorous, napalm, and high explosive bombs as accurately as a doctor selecting from the four main blood types for a blood transfusion. On abandoning the ship I was one of nine survivors on one of the two small caley floats. We clung to it all night with our hands grasping the ropes and only our heads above the water. The Captain clung to my shoulder for some time so did a boy of eighteen. Both were fatally wounded: Lieutenant H. P. Cobb, D.S.C. and Eric Higginbottom. So I wrote this poem and recalled the gratitude and happiness of those saved from the sea by an enemy patrol boat, given blankets, cognac, and medical treatment. That feeling between sailors which transcends war — of having saved and of having been saved after an action which commenced when three British Gun-boats entered a German coastal convoy.

22. *Looking Backward and Forward in Time of War*
This is another poem which looks at the past in the retrospect of the present. Eighty miles S.E. of Berlin, about half-way between Berlin and Wroclaw (Breslau) and nine miles from the Oder River in Silesia and what is now a part of Poland was the Air Force Camp, Stalag Luft III. To many in that camp the feeling about sand was that much more than 3/10ths of the earth's surface is made up of land. As tunnels moved forward foot by foot, ton after ton of sand was taken out of them and hidden in the compound. I was there during the building of the tunnel, "Harry" — it had an entrance shaft 28 feet deep, was 2 feet square, and 336 feet long. From that tunnel eighty prisoners escaped, four of whom were recaptured immediately on leaving the exit. This escape is described in Paul Brickhill's book, "Escape to Danger." Aidan Crawley who later became Under Secretary of State for Air in Mr. Attlee's Labour Government also wrote about it in "Escape from Germany." Himmler, Head of the Gestapo, mobilised 60,000 of the Home Guard.

23. *Sagan*
Tries to commemorate the event in a different way. For a long time I had kept the front page of the German newspaper, edited by the propaganda minister, Josef Goebbels. It showed pictures of Hitler arriving in triumph after the victories in Warsaw, Rotterdam, Belgrade, and I related the shooting of 50 prisoners of war at Sagan with these victories, with other cities prominent in the history of the war, and with our own atomic bombing of Nagasaki and Hiroshima.

24. *The Jungle Railway*
From Bangkok to Kanchanaburi by the river Khwae Noi, Thailand, on to Burma through 400 miles of undergrowth in dark green teak and bamboo jungle 60,000 Allied prisoners dwelt, 1942-43. The Japanese tried to build a railway from Bangkok to Rangoon as the preliminary step for an attack on India. On this episode of the war many

will remember who were fortunate to return — the tropical ulcers, beri-beri, malaria, cholera and malnutrition. The film "The Bridge on the River Kwai" shows something of their conditions. In addition to the allied soldiers there were over 100,000 Burmese, Tamils, Javanese, Malayans, and Chinese. According to Lord Russell more than half died. The spirit and the flesh, the jungle and the prison-camp — to endure the jungle as did Colonel Chapman, D.S.O., for almost $3\frac{1}{2}$ years as a fugitive in the Malayan jungle was beyond the normal human capacity for courage and endurance, to survive the prison-camp and the jungle, as did many, was to require a different mental attitude yet both were as gold in the fire. Assessing the conditions imposed by the Japanese a well-known social psychologist, Ruth Benedict, wrote a book, entitled, "The Sword and the Chrysanthemum." A historian no doubt would have considered the life of these prisoners as a retrogression in time to that of Herodotus who tabled the details of 100,000 slaves working 20 years to build the great Pyramids in Egypt, each block of which weighed $2\frac{1}{2}$ tons and required 40 men to move. Many of the boys on "The Jungle Railway" had been young conscripts. The poem tries to paint in words the mental sufferings of one who finally resolved his fears of death before he met God. One of 15,000.

25. *The Conquerors of Mars*
The theme of this poem is that the pen, like the great symbolic statue of peace, Christ of the Andes, is ultimately mightier than the sword. If I was asked the old question: What ten books would you choose if you had to spend a year alone on a desert island? I would include — "Hiroshima Diary," by Michihiko Hachiya.

26. *Duty to Country, or Let the Fires Go Out*
In 1938 I was a schoolboy at Allan Glen's, Scotland. As we played football in the playground instead of discussing the Code of Hammurabi, or, Einstein's theory of relativity, we talked about the possibility of war over the Sudeten

Crisis. Would Germany attack Czechoslovakia? The city of Prague under Benes and Jan Masaryk became to me a symbol of freedom in this century as it had been in the time of John Hus, and the sacrifice of Prague is depicted in the last few lines.

27. *The Escapees from the Prison Camp*
In Toronto among an audience mainly composed of ex-prisoners-of-war I saw a preview of the film "The Wooden Horse" and had never before felt such a tense atmosphere in a cinema. The film was about an escape modelled on the mythological Trojan Horse. The three escapees from the East Compound of Stalag Luft III who succeeded in reaching Britain via Sweden in 1943 were:
Flight Lieutenant E. E. Williams, M.C., R.A.F.
Lieutenant R. M. C. Codner, M.C., R.A.
Flight Lieutenant O. L. S. Philpot, M.C., D.F.C., R.A.F.
In the cinema I was with another well-known "kriegie," (Kriegsgefanger — prisoner-of-war) from Stalag Luft III, Wally Floody. Many times sand had collapsed on him when digging the tunnels in the North Compound from where three escapees reached Britain in "The Great Escape," two via Sweden and one:
Flight Lieutenant B. Van der Stok, R.A.F.
via Spain and Gibraltar . . ., in 1944.
Among other camps where I had been, and from others I heard of like Oflag 4C — Colditz, there was the same obsession of a few to escape. In Stalag 8B, 344, Lamsdorf, near Breslau, where over 20,000 soldiers were imprisoned, Group Captain Douglas Bader, D.S.O., D.F.C., went out on a working party but was brought back and the Germans threatened to take away his artificial legs. Many soldiers did escape and a few stayed with the Polish Underground Army of General Bor Komorovski. Several of those who tried to escape from these camps could have worn the crimson ribbon with the Royal Crown and Maltese Cross with the words inscribed — For Valour. One of the notable escapes was that of a Naval Officer

71

from Marlag O, who dressed in full Royal Navy uniform with the mere addition of a shoulder flash which read — Kralov Bulgrski Voyenno-Mrskoi Flot, or, Royal Bulgarian Navy, reached Britain via Sweden in 1943:

Lieutenant David James, M.B.E., D.S.C., R.N.V.R. This poem is for those escapees who paid forfeit for their attempts and illustrates my belief that when people die those nearest to them accompany them for a little of the way.

28. *Meditations on Remembrance Day at Niagara Falls*
Although Niagara Falls is only 160 ft. compared to the 3,212 ft. of Angel Waterfall in Venezuela and is perhaps not so spectacular as Victoria Falls, Niagara became more and more dear to me each time I walked from the Canadian side across Rainbow Bridge and round Goat's Island on the American side. One November 11, I stood during the two minutes of silence and thought of this poem. It is one I rewrote more than any other. To begin with it was in free verse and I submitted it to John Sutherland, the editor of Northern Review. It was later published in the Tower, editor, Miss Ida S. Groom, consultant editor, Dr. Lorne Pierce. The theme of the poem is the age-old tragedy of a love affair between two people, who through an accident of birth find that overnight their countries have become "the enemy" and are at war. Like many of my poems it is a three dimensional poem developing the past, the present, and the future. The poem opens with the lover returning to the place where he used to walk with his beloved. He feels that love is always a guiding star, and is inspired even in separation through trust in God. Mingled with these thoughts are the awakening hopes of the world for peace. He thinks reflectively of those who died in the First World War and how high the hope of men then had been that peace might reign. Finally he feels that in the carving of their names on the linden tree their love is united and immortal, that the name, Laura, like the Laura of Petrach, will always evoke her beauty.

29. *Elnora at 25*
   Was one of my first poems and written for one of my
   friends after I drove up from the seven locks of the
   Welland Canal to Toronto during Hurricane Hazel. My
   meeting and friendship with Elnora influenced my think-
   ing in the writing of these poems.

30. *The Birth of Sigrid*
   Was written for Sigrid, a little girl, twelve years old,
   whom I met in Montreal and drove to Toronto with her
   mother. The poem is my blessing on her by visualising
   her christening as a baby. She had long braided hair. Her
   English was only a few words none of which I remember.
   She, and her mother, now live in the United States.

31. *To Ann*
   When I lived in Toronto I used to play tennis on Centre
   Island. On returning home for a visit one of my friends
   asked me to visit his cousins. His uncle was extremely
   hospitable to me, and his cousin, Ann, showed me a picture
   of herself standing on the steps leading up to the Sacré
   Coeur Basilica, in Montmartre, Paris. I had stayed in a
   hotel for two weeks below that Basilica and the picture of
   the Sacré Coeur painted by Utrillo was an old one in my
   memory. I was very impressed by the snap of that teen-
   age girl, as she was then, and the great change in her as
   she is now.

32. *Jeanette Remembers*
   Jeanette is actually my name for Odette, one of the
   heroines of the French Resistance movement. Her romance
   with her war-time leader, Peter Churchill, led to marriage
   though subsequently they became divorced. Other heroines
   were: Yolande Beekman, Croix de Guerre, Andrée Borrel,
   Madeleine Damerment, Légion d'Honneur, C.d.G., Noor
   Inayat Khan, George Cross, C.d.G., Vera E. Leigh, Eliane
   Plewman, C.d.G., Diana Rowden, C.d.G., Violette Szabo,
   G.C., C.d.G., Sonia Olschonesky, Nancy Wake, G.C.,
   C.d.G. The road to crematorium, lethal injection and

shooting, often the fate of secret agents in France, Belgium, Holland, Denmark, Norway, Italy, Greece, Yugoslavia, Czechoslovakia, and Poland, amid catastrophe, betrayal and blunder, hunger, cold and loneliness, as well as heroism, has for the passer-by a core found in Donne's Devotions. "Any man's death diminishes me because I am involved in mankind." The names of eight women who died are remembered among others in St. Paul's Church, Knightsbridge, London, Britain, on the memorial tablet unveiled in 1948 by Princess Alice, Countess of Athlone.

33. *Chief of the Five Nations*

The first Indian I ever meet was Grey Owl in Sauchiehall Street, Glasgow. He was lecturing on the preservation of the beaver. Later I read about the Indians on Vancouver Island who were famous for their exchanges of gifts, pot-laches, and of the Haidas on the Queen Charlotte Islands who were celebrated for their totem poles, but like the famous Canadian painters who were unknown to me — Paul Kane, Cornelius Krieghof, Emily Carr, and the Group of Seven — I had never heard of the poet, Pauline Johnson, for whom there is a stone memorial and plaque in Stanley Park, Vancouver, B.C., and a plaque in the library of Brantford, Ontario, that is to say I had never heard of Pauline Johnson, grand-daughter of the Mohawk, Joseph Brant, until I came to Canada. In Brantford I must often have walked along the roads which she and her forefathers had walked along as paths. The Mohawks of New York State had always been friends of the British. They had fought against the French and in the savage Indian wars had practically exterminated the 50,000 Huron nation. They were loyal to the throne during the 1776-83 War and the 1812-14 war. Many of them left New York and settled on the grants of land which later became reserva-tions. One group went to Deseronto, another to what was later named after Joseph Brant, the city of Brantford. These reservations were constantly encroached upon by white settlers.

34. *The Immigrant*
The hope of all immigrants is for a golden future for their families. There is a saying, "that it takes three generations to make a Canadian."

35. *The Old St. Lawrence Market in Toronto*
The Indian name for Toronto is often said to be, "the meeting place of the nations!" Here General Simcoe, the first Lieutenant Governor of Upper Canada settled with his Welsh wife on what is now probably four blocks of the present city. He built Fort York and named the settlement York after the Duke of York. Much of the activity of the people during the following years and up to the present was centred round the St. Lawrence market.

36. *The Islands of Toronto*
I spent many happy hours on the islands — canoeing, tennis, walking — during my 18 months there and always felt relaxed on returning to the city.

37. *Casa Loma*
Was built by Sir Henry Pellatt one of the foremost financiers in Canada during the end of the Victorian era. He was generous and enthusiastic. His hope was that when the Royal Family visited the second largest country in the world, Canada, they would live in the Castle. He spent $2,000,000, 1911-14 in the building of Casa Loma. He received financial losses in the 1930's and for the last few years of his life Casa Loma passed into the possession of the city. I used to live two blocks away and at nights Casa Loma was illuminated when used by the Kiwanis Club for dances or wedding receptions.

38. *Clear the Way*
A comment on careless reckless drivers who drive with an instinctive objective like geese flying at over 29,000 feet, or loons diving 160 feet into the water.

39. *The Kirkintilloch and the Obernkirchen Children's Choirs in Canada.*

These two choirs are my favourite children's choirs. When the Kirkintilloch Choir came to Toronto I was working in Guelph. I drove the seventy miles in to hear them and after driving through the mist I arrived back in Guelph at 2 a.m. The little town of Kirkintilloch is about four miles from Stepps, and it was in the Sunday school hall of St. Andrew's United Church of Scotland in Stepps that I first heard them. The beauty of the lilting Scottish voices and the swing of the Scottish kilts were never more impressive. I heard the Obernkirchen Children's Choir in Massey Hall, Toronto, and started to write this poem that evening in a Honey Dew Restaurant on Yonge Street.

40. *The Children at Mont Tremblant*

I spent a week's holiday ski-ing at Mont Tremblant. The snowy grandeur of the mountains could not be excelled. I used to go up the North side in the morning, ski over the top, and spend the rest of the day on the South side, or vice versa. I felt as if I had a billion dollars and that every minute was worth a dollar.

41. *An Interpretation of Destiny*

Of the Nine Muses my choice would be Clio, the Muse of History, mainly because I have certain bonds with the past, and I used to tease a friend by calling her Clio. Here I have sketched a scene from Galilee. I wrote it at the time I became a member of the United Church of Canada. The last line is my prayer, "That I may live with Christ in me" to fill my hands in any place where I might be. Most people of a Christian background have at some-time shared the feeling of Moses expressed in Exodus 4:10, "O my Lord, I am not eloquent, neither heretofore nor since Thou has spoken unto Thy servant; but I am slow of speech and of a slow tongue."

42. *Youth, To-day and Yesterday*

Looks at the bloom of youth, wonders what the future

will hold in store and what they will return for the gift of life. Sir Wilfred Grenfell of Labrador said, "The service we render to others is really the rent we pay for our room on this earth. It is obvious that man is himself a traveller that the purpose of this world is not, 'to have and to hold,' but, 'to give and to serve.' There can be no other meaning."

43. *The Harbour*
Is trying to show the anxiety of a sailor's wife for her husband's safety during a storm. It is written in the form of a rondeau.

44. *The Balance Sheet*
Two of the greatest singers I have heard are Marian Anderson and Paul Robeson. One I heard in Vancouver the other in Toronto, at the old Georgia Auditorium and at Massey Hall. The two rhymes in this poem represent debits and credits and these two people both know the debit and credit sides of life. The poem is a plea to help the hungry peoples of the world and not to forget about them as if they lived as far away as the Nile and the Amazon, as rivers which will never be united.

45. *The Pioneer's Farm*
One of the pictures I remember from my school books is that of "The Angelus" by François Millet. It shows a French farmer and his wife praying in reverent love of God on hearing the church bells calling them to prayer as if with the words, "Though I speak with the tongues of men and of angels, and have not love, I am become as sounding brass." This poem is a pastoral poem and may represent a little of the life of some of my forefathers, who for the past few generations were probably farmers, at least my grandfathers, three uncles, and cousins galore in Scotland, Canada, and New Zealand.

It concludes this series of poems with the thought:
And there youth learned the simple chore:
Kinship with God and the half wild deer,

To walk along the stubble floor,
To spend one's self for other's cheer
Throughout the year.

With that thought in mind I recall that in October, 1957, the World Youth Festival was held in Moscow, U.S.S.R., and that members of the Celtic Ballet from Glasgow were represented. I almost went as an outside observer. If I had gone I would certainly have accepted the invitation of the Chinese to other delegates to spend five weeks in China for there are two attitudes towards the cold war in the world to-day:

1. Differences are irreconcilable. One side must dominate the other. War is inevitable.

2. Understanding towards nuclear disarmament can be achieved step by step through peaceful negotiations so that both sides will be victorious for all countries have something to take and something to give.

I believe in the second school of thought and that everyone can contribute in some degree to a better understanding among the peoples of the world. A minister of the Christian church acts by divine commission and also as the representative of the believing community so the statesman represents the people. Yet it is for us the people to use our limited talents in our different ways for the good of mankind. That is the hope of the Christian, the Buddhist, the Confucianist, the Hindu, the Jew, the Moslem, and all the other people on the earth. May we not fail our children's children by not destroying the seeds of a 3rd World War. In the hundreds of prison camps during the 2nd World War there was a cross-section of humanity as evidenced, for example, by the imprisonment of:

Reverend Dr. Caskie, O.B.E., the minister of the Scottish church in Paris.

Major John Dodge, D.S.O., D.S.C., M.C., a Lieutenant Colonel in the 1st World War who was awarded the D.S.O. and D.S.C. for gallantry at the Dardanelles, who was Chairman of the Ends of the Earth Club, and who in the 2nd World War escaped five times from his guards, escapes which included Stalag Luft III and Sachsenhausen Concentration Camp.

Captain the Earl Haig — the son of the British Commander-in-Chief of the 1st World War, Field Marshal Douglas Haig of Bemersyde.

Earl Harewood — then Lieutenant Viscount Lascelles, a cousin of Queen Elizabeth.

Captain Charles Hazlitt Upham, V.C. and Bar.

General Papagos — Commander-in-Chief of the Greek Army who with 16 Greek Divisions pinned down for several months in Albania 27 Italian Divisions.

O. Nansen — the son of the Norwegian Explorer.

Sylvia Salvensen — a friend of the Norwegian Royal Family.

Princess Matilda of Italy.

General Garibaldi — the grandson of the Italian Liberator.

Prince Philip of Hesse.

The relatives of Colonel Claus von Stauffenburg — the man who had left the time bomb in his brief case under the table in the wooden hut at Hitler's Rastenburg H.Q.

And many others — rich and poor, literate and illiterate.

No matter what wealth or fame a person possessed, the prison camp removed it all and man was revealed to man as having the same basic hopes, fears, aspirations and anxieties. There was learned directly, or, indirectly, the effect of hunger, disease, and inequality on one's outlook on life, the effect on displaced persons of delay and uncertainty.

Now that all these memories are of another generation it is still the duty of all who have experienced war, of all who have been civilian internees, hostages, or, prisoners of war, not to be tepid and indifferent to the problems of the world, but to be active for peace in the solution of hunger and nuclear disarmament. May the Utopia of vision, realism, and resolution in international understanding occur in the 20th Century. Yet if it does not, may the path to the 21st Century be widened as we walk slowly and uncertainly along united in strength by the memory of the past like a remembered dream that is drawn from strange and great people.

> To walk along the stubble floor,
> To spend one's self for other's cheer
> Throughout the year.